英語で学ぶ
プライマリーケア

Primary Care

A practical English communication course
for Nurses and healthcare workers

西牟田 祐美子 編著
Yumiko Nishimuta

講談社

執筆者一覧

編著者

西牟田《にしむた》 祐美子《ゆみこ》

（1, 12章）

岐阜保健大学看護学部看護学科教授

著者（執筆順）

土井《どい》やすこ Yancy

（2, 3章）

エルウィン・カブリド

（Erwin Cabrido ; 4, 5, 6章）

ナイレー・アン・キーナン

（Ngaire Anne Keenan ; 7, 9, 10, 11章）

リサ・マンジヤック

（Lisa Mandziak ; 8, 13, 14, 15章）

はじめに

看護大学はもともと数が少なく，1989年度にはわずか11大学で，入学者の数も500人程度でした。ところが看護師不足を背景に年々増加し続けて，2019年（平成31年）では288大学に看護学部が設置されました。現在は横ばい状態とはいえ，根強い人気を誇っています。また，看護の専門学校も現在250校以上あるといわれています。

外国語の授業は1年生，2年生の教養科目として，また専門基礎という枠の中でどの看護学部でも，また看護学校でも，2または4単位で行われています。その中でも，英語はどの大学・看護学校でも教えられています。

2020年は，新型コロナウイルスが引き起こしたパンデミックにより，日本のみならず世界中がこの感染症の脅威に現在もおびえています。また2020年は看護の母で，患者の衛生的な環境について説いたフローレンス・ナイチンゲールの生誕200年の年にもあたります。現在，国はコロナ患者の増加を受け，離職した看護師を呼び戻すべく，要請補助を行い始めました。

看護職に対する熱い視線はこれまでの人気をさらに高めています。また，このパンデミックのなか，一層グローバルなコミュニケーション能力が医療，看護職，およびコメディカルの職種に求められてきています。

医師や看護師，患者とその家族，病院という組織で働く人たちの中で英語での意思伝達を助けることができれば，外国人の患者さんの精神的な不安や苦痛を少しでも軽減でき，治療も進むことでしょう。

私は実際に看護英語を教える大学現場で，ネイティブの先生方と折に触れて看護学生のコミュニケーション能力を高める授業，教科書について情報交換してきました。しかし，その先生方より，実際に使いたい看護英語の教科書がなかなか見当たらないという声を聴き，自分たちが実際に使いたいと思うような，コミュニケーションに使える看護英語の教科書を作りました。

コンセプトとして，1冊をストーリー仕立てにすることにしました。舞台は日本国内の病院です。毎章ストーリーが展開していき，読者（学生）は，それを漫画，ダイアログ，ブログ，ショートメッセージのやり取りなどから，主人公たちが今どんな状況なのかを知ることができます。文法のポイントも各章毎に説明し，さまざまな角度から学習できるようになっています。

各章始めの4コマ漫画には，その章のキーセンテンスとなるセリフが盛り込まれ，英語が苦手な学生も，大人数のクラスでも，一人一人がビジュアル的に状況を理解でき，また主人公たちに感情移入しやすい設定となっています。読者は主人公たちと病院内のさまざまな科や人々に出会いながら，英語でのコミュニケーション，病院内外で使えるボキャブラリーを，クイズ，ゲーム等も交えながら楽しく学習していくことができます。

本書の執筆者全員が外国での医療を受けた経験者という特性も活かし，リーディングでは，各自が実際に体験したユーモア溢れるエピソードが読むことができます。

最後に，授業の合間を縫って，企画，構成，執筆を進めてきた著者の先生方，企画からずっと助言，応援してくださったジェームズ・グラッドストーン様，本書のネイティブチェックや，別冊の日本語訳に取り組んでくださった清水ケリー様，そしてこのパンデミックのさなか出版することができましたのは，講談社サイエンティフィクの三浦洋一郎様をはじめ，皆様のご支援によるものです。心より感謝申し上げます。

2020年7月

西牟田祐美子

Contents

四コマ漫画：西牟田　誠
本文イラスト：TSスタジオ

Introduction

We're going to visit a hospital in Japan where several foreign nationals are having their health problems attended to.

One of them is Tom – he's a young man on his travels from the UK who's been involved in an accident and hurt his leg. Luckily for him there is a student nurse Ann who can interpret to him as she speaks good English. Nurse Sato and Nurse Tanaka are two of the staff who will be looking after Tom while he is in hospital, and Dr. Kawada is the surgeon, Ken the English speaking Radiologist.

We also meet a few more people who have come to have their problems diagnosed and sorted and eavesdrop on the patient's contacts with their friends and families.

Let's hope they all get better soon and Tom and Ann can have maybe more than patient and career relationship....

Tom

Ann

Ken

Dr. Kawada

Chapter 1

Emergency and Vital signs

Take a look at the Manga!

1 Useful Vocabulary

- terrible
- finger
- numbers
- vital signs (blood pressure, pulse, body temperature)
- thermometer
- sphygmomanometer
- stethoscope
- IV stand
- stretcher
- ambulance

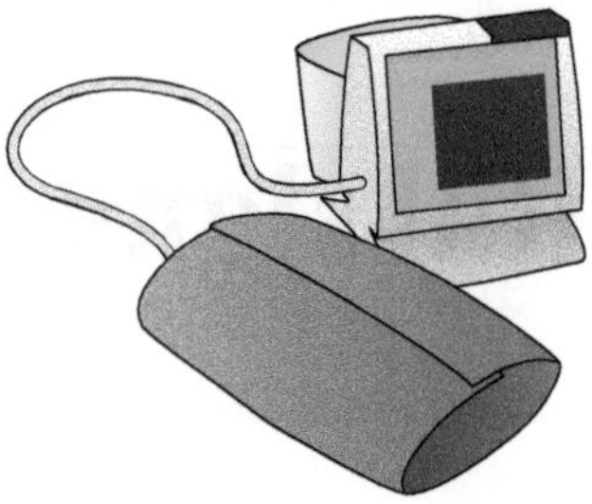

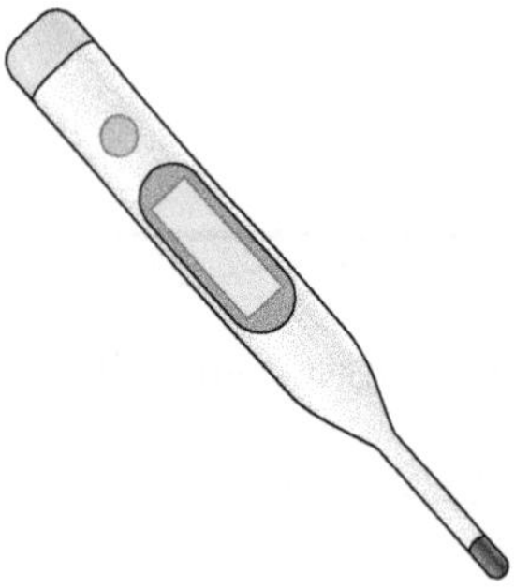

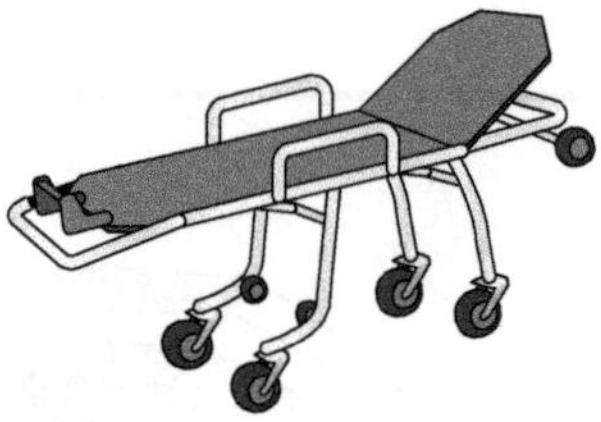

② Role-play practice 1

Work in pairs and ask how he/she is and why?

Q: How are you doing?

A: Excellent

Great

Good

So-so

Not so good

Bad

Terrible

Awful

Ask your partner how he/she is, and why.

Q: Why?

A1: Because I saw my friend and we went out and talked a lot.

A2: Oh I don't know exactly, but maybe because I worked too long.

③ Useful expressions

1. Fingers

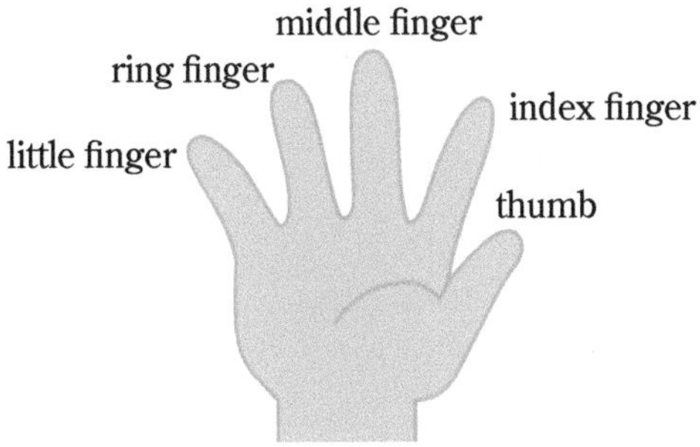

2. Numbers

- one
- two
- three
- four
- five
- six
- seven
- eight
- nine
- ten
- eleven
- twelve
- thirteen
- fourteen
- fifteen
- sixteen
- twenty
- twenty-one
- twenty-two
- hundred
- hundred one
- hundred two
- one hundred twenty-three

Exercise

Ten plus fifteen is ________.

Twenty minus eleven is _______.

Forty-four times seven is ________.

Twelve divided by three is _______.

Work in pairs

E.g. Q: What's 66 plus 18?

A: 66 plus 18 is 84.

plus	minus	times	divided by
66+18=	18−9=	7×2=	24÷6=
23+49=	24−8=	15×3=	66÷3=
38+43=	96−45=	62×5=	34÷17=
19+7=	86−69=	76×7=	880÷22=

4 Grammar Focus

- What's your name?
  Where are you?/ am I?
  Where are you from?
  How are you feeling? OK/ Terrible
  How many fingers? Five! / six?

  Can you speak Japanese?
  Are you OK? Yes/ No
  Do you have a family here?

- Establishing Vital signs (Numbers)

- You have to make sure that his /her airway is secured.
  Q: How is his blood pressure?
  A: His high blood pressure is 128/ the lowest is 86
  Q: How is his pulse?
  A: His pulse is 82.
  His pulse is elevated.

  Q: How is his body temperature?
  A: His temperature is 36.7.(Celsius)
  His temperature dropped.

5 Role-play practice 2

You become an ambulance person and hand over a patient and report the vital sign to the hospital staff.

Example
Man (car accident)
Airway is secured.
Blood pressure is 178/70.
Pulse 99
Temperature 37.6

Q: How is his blood pressure?
A: His high blood pressure is 178/ the lowest is 70

Q: How is his pulse?
A: His pulse is 99.

Q: How is his body temperature?
A: His temperature is 37.6(Celsius).

1. The man was in an accident
   His airway is secured.
   His blood pressure is 178/88.
   Pulse is 99.
   His body temperature is 37.5

2. woman (fire)
   Airway is not secured.
   Blood pressure 177/70
   Pulse 104
   Temperature 38.0
   Burn

3. Boy (drown)
   Airway secured
   Blood pressure 130/67
   Pulse 110
   Temperature 37.3

6 Listening

Listen to the following conversation and answer the questions. Then compare your answer to your partner's.

Doctor in ER: Tell me his vital signs please. Is his airway secured?
Ambulance person: Yes, we secured his airway. His blood pressure is 136/100.
Doctor: Ok, great. Pulse?
A: 97
Doctor: Good good, How about his body temperature?
A: 37.2.
Doctor: Thank you.

Exercise

Patient's vital signs

1. Blood pressure?
2. Pulse?
3. Temperature ?
4. His airway secured?

7 Pair work

Interview 2 classmates and write their answers.

Q1. What is your name?
Partner 1 ______________________________
Partner 2 ______________________________

Q2. Where do you live?
Partner 1 ______________________________
Partner 2 ______________________________

Q3. Do you have any brothers or sisters?
Partner 1 ______________________________
Partner 2 ______________________________

Q4. Do you have a pet?

Partner 1 ______________________________

Partner 2 ______________________________

Q5. What do you do in your free time?

Partner 1 ______________________________

Partner 2 ______________________________

Q6. What's your future dream?

Partner 1 ______________________________

Partner 2 ______________________________

Q7. ______________________________? (Make your own question)

Partner 1 ______________________________

Partner 2 ______________________________

Q8. ______________________________? (Make your own question)

Partner 1 ______________________________

Partner 2 ______________________________

8 Dialogue

Here is Ann(an interpreter and nursing student) and her mother (American)'s conversation.

M: Hi Honey, what's up?

A: Well, I am tired. I saw an English boy in ER. He doesn't seem very good. His blood pressure is very high.

M: Oh, God. Does he live in Japan?

A: I am not sure. A tourist, I guess.

M: How old is he?

A: Maybe in his early 20s? I hope he will get better.

M: I'm sure he will.

9 Role-play practice 3

Read the dialogue in pairs, and answer the following questions.

1. Who they are talking about?
2. How are his vital signs?
3. How old is he?

10 Short Writing exercise

Ann accidentally found Tom's blog!

Tom's blog
Name: Tom Hill
Country: UK
Interests: traveling, currently in Japan
My favourite is banana smoothie!

Now write about your own profile, using your photos, avatar, etc.

Name:
Country
Interests, hobbies,
Favourite food

11 Game 'Who is your teacher?'

Work in groups of 4 or 5. In a group, discuss what kind of questions you will want to ask your teacher for example, "Does he/she have a child?" Etc (Discussion is all in English).
Then choose one question and ask this in class. .....GroupA

The other groups (Group B, for example) discuss and answer the question as if they are the teacher.
So Group C answers Group B's question.

The group guessing most correctly is the winner!

Now individually ask any questions of your teacher.

12 Extra Reading

Of course here in Japan I can't understand much of what is happening on the ward, which is very different from last time I had to be in hospital in the UK. Maybe there I understood too much.

I was in A&E for the night, following a head injury and hoping to get some sleep. But for what seemed like hours there was a constant plaintive cry from a male patient in the adjoining ward:-

"Give me a pill."

This was obviously keeping others awake, as finally another voice called out:-
"For God's sake somebody give him a pill!"

It was funny and sad at the same time.

I'm sure the nurses would have liked to give him a pill, but if it wasn't on his medication list, I suppose they couldn't.

*A&D: accident and emergency

Questions

1. Why was the person in the hospital in UK?
2. What did the male patient want?
3. Finally did he get what he want?

Chapter 2

At the Radiology

1 Useful Vocabulary

- painful
- car accident
- outpatient reception
- radiology
- What a relief!
- corridor

2 Grammar points

Role-play practice

Just a word with rising intonation can work as a question.

Q: (What is) Your name/address/postal code?

A: Tom/1-2 Ueno/123-456

Q: (Are you) O.K?

A: Yes, (I am ok)/well, not really.

Q: (Is this) Your handkerchief/pen/student card?

A: (Yes,) thanks.

Departments and the Specialists

internal medicine/doctor, general practitioner, physician

surgery/surgeon

orthope(a)dics/orthope(a)dist, orthope(a)dic surgeon

pediatrics/pediatrician

obstetrics/obstetrics

gynecology/gynecologist

ob-gyn/ob-gyn specialist

dermatology/dermatologist

urology/urologist

psychiatry/psychiatrist

neurology/neurologist

radiology/radiologist

anesthesiology/anesthesiologist

dentistry/dentist

cardiology/cardiologist

heart surgery/heart surgeon

ophthalmology/ophthalmologist

eye clinic/eye specialist

otorhinolaryngology/otorhinolaryngologist

ear, nose, & throat clinic: ENT/ear, nose and throat specialist

Useful expression 'direction'

Use your hand to show a direction to go.

Repeat the direction you heard.

Turn right/left.

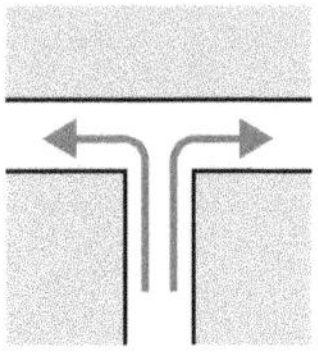

Go straight.

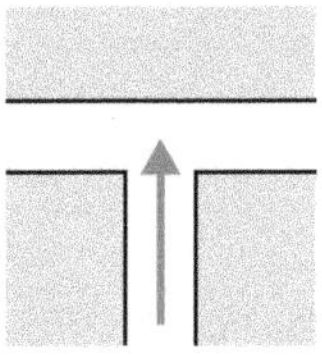

A is next to B.

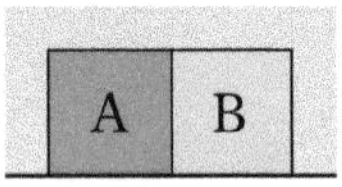

A is between B and C.

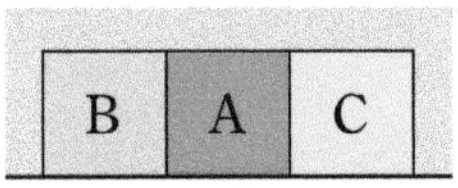

A is across from B.

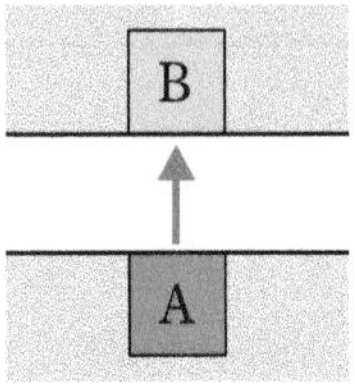

A is in front/back of B.

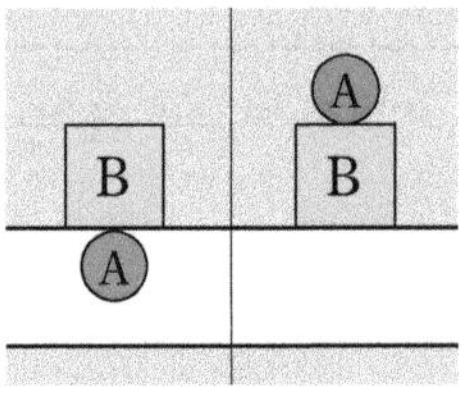

A is on the left/right.

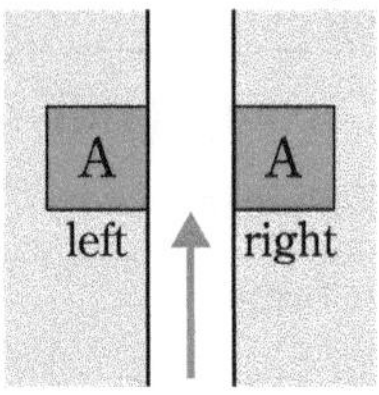

Facilities in a hospital

reception	pharmacy	urinalysis lab	blood lab
accounting	restaurant	coffee shop	kitchenette
laundry	rooftop	elevator	ATM
ER	hospital morgue	heliport	automatic outpatient
janitor's office	convenience store	(no) smoking area	visitor's launge
operation room	rehabilitation room	vending machine	

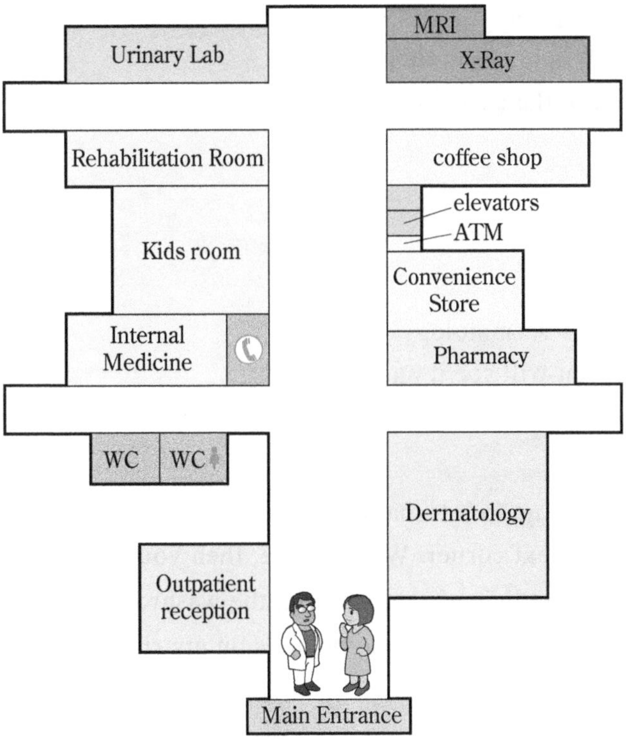

3 Dialogue

Listen to the following conversations.

Tom is on a stretcher in the hospital. Tom, Ann, and a nurse are heading for radiology.

Ann: What's your name?
Tom: Tom.
Ann: Are you in pain?
Tom: Yes. It's very painful.
Ann: Please try not to move. We'll take you to the radiology.
Here we are, Tom.
Ken(Radiologist): Car accident, right? Can you sit up?
Tom: I don't think I can but I'll try.
Nurse Tanaka: Ken, you speak good English!
Ken: I went on a working holiday in Australia a few years ago.
Tom: What a relief! I don't speak Japanese very well.
Ann: All right, then. I will go back to the outpatient reception.

At the outpatient reception
A hospital visitor: Where is the shop?
Ann: It's at the end of the corridor.
The visitor: Thanks.

outpatient reception

Outpatient1: Where is dermatology?
Ann: Go straight. You will see it on your right.
Outpatient: Thanks.

Outpatient2: I'd like to go to internal medicine.
Ann: Turn left at the next corner. Walk a little, then you will see a men's washroom on your left. Internal medicine is across from the washroom.
Outpatient2: So, you mean internal medicine is on my right.
Ann: Yes, that's right.

Woman: Is there an elevator?
Ann: Yes. Do you see a convenience store over there?
Woman: Yes.
Ann: There are two elevators next to it.

4 Pair work

Practice how to show locations with your partner.

Where is ____________________?	I'd like to go to ____________________.
Do you have _________________?	Is (Are) there _____________________?

Ask your partner his/her occupation.

What do you do?	I am a(an) ______________________.

1 doctor	2 nurse	3 pharmacist	4 midwife
5 paramedic	6 receptionist	7 director	8 professor

5 Ann's Text messaging with Sister

Read the following text messaging.

Writing

Write in regular English.

How r u? ( )?

I am g8. ( )

LOL ( )

IC ( )

CU ( )

tmrw ( )

ICU ( ) 【Riddle】

6 Game

Department BINGO

Fill in the 25 squares with names of departments or facilities in a hospital.
Take turns saying a word from the Bingo sheet you created. You can use some words twice.

reception	pharmacy	urinalysis lab	blood lab
accounting	restaurant	coffee shop	vending machine
kitchenette	laundry	rooftop	elevator
ATM	ER	hospital morgue	heliport
automatic outpatient	janitor's office	visitor's launge	convenience store
(no) smoking area	rehabilitation room	operation room	

B	I	N	G	O

7 Reading/Listening comprehension

Read (Listen to) the telephone conversation and answer the questions below.

Asking locations on the phone

Female: ABC General Hospital, how can I help you?

Male: This is Michael Brown, Tom Carpenter's friend. I heard he was brought there after a car accident. Am I right?

F: We are sorry, Mr. Brown. We are not allowed to answer those questions to protect our patients' privacy. But if you come here, we can search for the name you mentioned and if we find the name, we will let the patient know that he has a visitor.

M: I see. How can I get there? I am coming from downtown by bus.

F: Please take the No.200 bus that leaves from Central Bus Terminal. It's about a 15-minute ride. Get off the bus at EFG shopping mall bus stop. Go into the shopping mall from the main entrance and just go straight to the other side of the entrance until you see North Entrance. Leave the EFG shopping mall and turn right.

M: Let me write that down. Just a moment.   Thanks. I am ready.

F: Leave EGF shopping mall and turn right. Then, go straight ahead 2 blocks, you will see ABC General Hospital on your left. It is about a 5-minute walk.

M: Thank you so much. You speak good English. Will you be there?

F: I'm not sure, I will be finishing my shift soon, sir.

M: Oh, ok. Thanks. Bye.

Questions

1. What is the woman's job?
2. What did the man want to know at first?
3. Why did the woman say, "I am not allowed to answer those questions"?
4. How long does it take to get to ABC General Hospital from Central Bus Terminal?
5. Draw a rough map from the main entrance of EFG shopping mall to ABC General Hospital.

8 Extra reading

Read the article below and discuss your experiences in finding out a washroom with your classmates.

What is the most frequently asked location in the world? Is it a Station? Actually, it is quite likely to be the "TOILET". It is obviously one of the most important rooms for everyone.

Did you know that there are so many words for 'toilet' in English? How would you say it? If you call it *toilet* in the U.S.A., some may think you mean the toilet seat itself. People call it *restroom, washroom, bathroom, lavatory, W.C.*, and so many more. Some may call it *ladies' room or men's room*. When my friend called it a *loo*, I didn't understand what she meant. So, she rephrased, "I'd like to wash my hands."

Japan has recently started to see more patients from overseas. Not only receptionists but also all the medical workers ought to know many words that mean "toilet" in case they are the only ones that might be around when someone is urgently in need.

Chapter 3

X-ray and Bones

1 Useful Vocabulary

- by myself
- necessary
- angle
- anterior compartment
- internally
- orthopedic surgery
- spiral fracture
- certainly
- experience
- ouch
- swell/swelled/ swollen
- bleed
- needle manometer, internal pressure
- right away
- compartment syndrome
- shortly

2 Grammar points

Useful expressions 1

Let me help you.

Gosh!

No kidding!

Stay still.

Please be patient.

Useful expressions 2 'Comparative expressions'

It is painful.

It is more painful.

It is much more painful.

It is the most painful.

Choose one or more possible answer(s).

Dr. Smith is a great / greater / the greatest doctor.

My blood pressure is normally low / lower / the lowest than this.

Good sleep can be important / more important / the most important than eating.

It was difficult / more difficult / the most difficult decision I had ever made.

I believe the preservative treatment is good / better / the best.

Useful expressions 3 'Present and Past participles'

a/the broken machine	a/the machine that was broken yesterday
a/the crying girl	a/the girl crying in her mother's arms
a/the bleeding limb	a/the limb bleeding just a little

3 Dialogue

Ken: Can you put your right leg here?

Tom: I don’t think I can do it by myself.

Ken: Let me help you. But it might be more painful, as we move it.

Tom: Gosh! This is the most painful experience in my life.

Ken: X-ray is necessary. Are you ready? (moves his leg)

Tom: Uh! Ouch!

Ken: Stay still.

Ken: One more time. Another image from a different angle is necessary.

Tom: No kidding! It’s starting to hurt more! Ouch!

Ken: All done. The anterior compartment is probably damaged and bleeding internally. Needle manometer will be necessary to check the internal pressure.

Tom: That sounds much more painful.

Ken: Please be patient.

Ken: Take Tom to Orthopedic Surgery right away. And tell Dr. Kawada that *this is a spiral fracture which could cause a compartment syndrome.*

Nurse Tanaka: Certainly.

On the way to Orthopedic Surgery

Nurse Tanaka: Don’t worry, Tom. It won’t take too long. Dr. Kawada will see you shortly.

Tom; O.K.

4 Pair work

Give an order to touch his/her body part, using following patterns.

Student A: Please point to your (　　　　　). Student B: Action
Student A: Where is your (　　　　　　　)? Student B: Here
Student A: Where does it hurt? Student B: My (　　　　　) hurt(s).

Parts of the Body

Head

head face hair forehead eye(s) eyelid(s) eyebrow(s) eyelash(es) nose nostril(s) cheek(s) ear(s) lip(s) mouth gum(s) tooth(teeth) tongue jaw chin neck throat tonsil(s) uvula

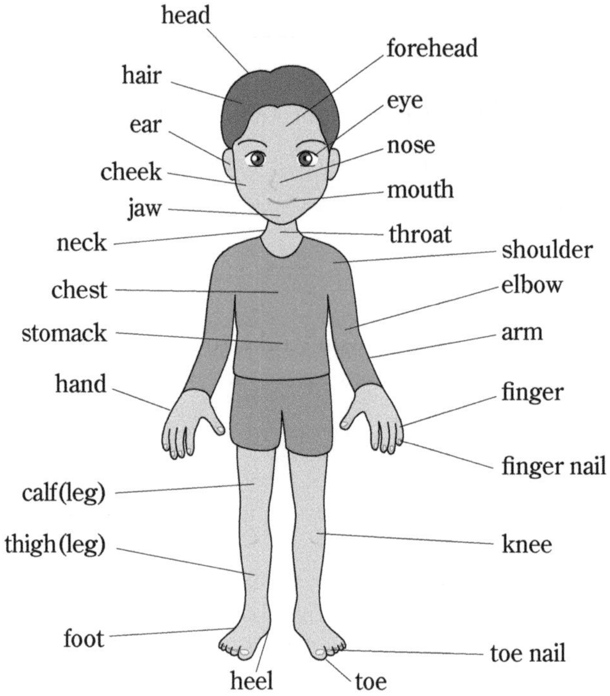

Limbs

shoulder(s) arm(s) elbow(s) wrist(s) hand(s) palm(s) finger(s) nail(s) leg(s) foot(feet) thigh(s) knee(s) shin(s) calf(calves) ankle(s) heel(s) sole(s) toe(s)

Trunk

chest breast(s) abdomen stomach (tummy) waist back upper back lower back buttocks

Bones

skull shoulder blade spine humerus(humeruses) thighbone(s)/femur(s)

5 Writing

Write down the questions you need to play the game below.

Whose profile is this? Game (Actual name should not be written)

- Write your future profile on a piece of paper without your name.
- Mix them up and choose one of them.
- Start asking questions to find out whose profile you have.
- Keep changing your partner until you find out whose profile it is.
  When time is up, count how many profiles you indentified.

6 Game

Play 'Simon says' with body parts in class.

Refer to the expressions given in the pair work section.

7 Reading/Listening comprehension

Read (Listen to) the following conversations and answer the questions

1.

M: What's the matter, Nancy?

F: I think John has a fever.

M: Really? Yes, he is quite hot.

F: Can you give us a ride to the clinic?

M: Of course.

F: Thanks. I'll get a baby sling right away.

Q&A

1. What is the problem?
2. What department are they going to visit?

2.

F: Ouch! My left elbow still hurts.

M: Can you move your left arm?

F: Yes, I can. But it is painful when I move it.

M: Did you see a doctor?

F: No. I thought it would be all right soon.

M: I guess you should see a doctor.

Q&A

1. What department should this woman visit?
2. Why didn't this woman visit a doctor sooner?

3

F: Hello. This is Jane Carpenter.

M: Hi, Jane. David speaking. What can I do for you?

F: I will visit you around 4 p.m. tomorrow after seeing Dr. Noguchi.

M: You are calling to confirm that the drugs you need are in stock, right? We are sorry that you had to come again last time.

F: No problem. If I feel well this afternoon, I'll bake some lemon pies and you can have them tomorrow.

M: That sounds great. I look forward to seeing you. Take care, Jane.

Q&A

1. Where is this man working?
2. When will this woman visit David?

8 Related Topic 1

You are working at a middle-sized hospital in Japan.
You are not too busy but still you have many things to do.
You find a person who you think is from overseas. He/She seems to be in trouble or in need of help.
Answer the questions below. Choose the most likely answer.

Q1 What would you do?
- a. Go through without doing anything.
- b. Stop and think what to do.

Q2 Would you do or say something to the person?
- a. Yes
- b. No

Q3 What would you most likely do?
- a. I would call the person in charge of those cases.
- b. I would ask the person if he/she needs help.

Q4 What would you say to the person?
- a. I would say "Daijoubudesuka" in Japanese.
- b. I would say "OK?" for example.

Use the answers of Q1-4 as the starting point to think about what to do.
There are no correct or incorrect answers. Make a list of situations where 'a' would be more appropriate and 'b' would be more appropriate. Share your answers with your classmates. Discuss why the answer would be appropriate or inappropriate.

- Medical workers are usually busy.
- A person in trouble can be in an urgent situation.
- Medical workers work as a team.
- There are helpful devices such as smartphones or translation apps.

Think flexibly and critically. Be wise and make yourself a better medical worker.

Topic 2

It is important to show that you are/are not following the on-going conversation.

★What would you say or do when you understand the conversation well?

I see.

Yes.

O.K.

Add more expressions you can think of. ______________________

Actions?

★What would you say or do when you understand the conversation roughly but you want to confirm if your understanding is correct or not?

Do you mean that I should turn left at the next corner and then I will find an elevator on my right?

Let me confirm the decision.

So, the operation can be tomorrow. Am I right?

Add more expressions you can think of. ______________________

Actions?

★What would you say or do when you don't understand well?

Pardon?

What is endocrinology?

What do you mean by "same difference"?

Add more expressions you can think of. ______________________

Actions?

Chapter 4

Preparation for an operation, names of body parts

1 Useful Vocabulary

- acute
- limb
- chronic
- amputate
- fasciotomy

② Grammar Focus

To swell: to become larger or rounder in size, typically as a result of an accumulation of fluid.

As a verb:

Present Tense	*Body parts* ***swell*** *from injury or inflammation.*
Past Tense	*My ankle* ***swelled*** *up to the size of a softball.*
As an adjective:	*The patient's body might be* ***swollen*** *after surgery.*

Can and Can't

Can means able to do something or that something is possible.

Example: I can walk without any problems.

Can't (cannot) means unable to do something or that something is impossible.

Example: I can't eat or drink anything the night before the surgery.

PAIN ASSESSMENT TOOL

One of the most common pain assessment tools is the Wong-Baker Faces Pain Rating Scale. This simple scale was originally developed for children. However, it can be used with all patients from 3 years old and above.

(Wong-Baker FACES Foundation (2020). Wong-Baker FACES® Pain Rating Scale. Retrieved [3/17/2020] with permission from http://www.WongBakerFACES.org.)

Other useful expressions of pain in the Wong-Baker Faces Pain Rating Scale:

0 No pain
2 Mild Pain
4 Moderate Pain
6 Severe Pain
8 Very Severe Pain
10 Worst Possible Pain

Example expression:

1. My fingers are swollen. I can't move them.
2. My tonsils are swollen. I can't eat.
3. My leg hurts a little bit, but I can walk.
4. I can't see anything because my eyes are swollen.
5. My throat hurts a whole lot, so I can't eat or drink.

Common Body Parts (復習)

Fill in the blanks.

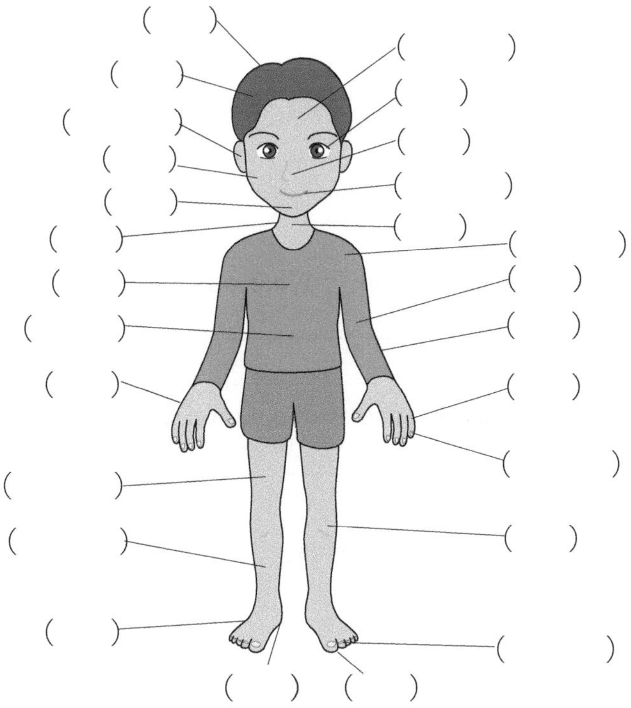

3 Listening

Listen to the following interview and fill in the blanks with the missing words. Practice the dialogue with a partner.

Ann: Is Tom going to be ok after the surgery?

Nurse Sato: We cannot make any promises, but we will do our best! It's good that he can undergo fasciotomy at once.

Ann: Fasci... what?

Nurse Sato: Fasciotomy. It is ________ to relieve the swelling or pressure of an area of tissue or muscle in cases of acute compartment syndrome.

Ann: I see. What happens if he cannot have the surgery immediately?

Nurse Sato: In cases where the patient could not go to a hospital soon, the muscles might suffer ________ damage and in extreme cases the limb may have to be amputated.

Ann: Amputated? Does that mean the limb will be ________ ? Oh dear!

Nurse Sato: In _____ cases only. Don't worry. Dr. Kawada is an expert surgeon. She has treated many patients like Tom who did not delay going to the hospital.

Ann: I'm glad you said that. I hope Tom can get back on _______ his feet soon.

4 Pair work

Interview 2 classmates and write their answers.

Q1. Have you been to the hospital lately? What was wrong?

Partner 1 ____________________

Partner 2 ____________________

Q2. What was the worst pain you have ever experienced?

Partner 1 ____________________

Partner 2 ____________________

Q3. What do you do when you have a headache?

Partner 1 ____________________

Partner 2 ____________________

Q4. Do you think women can tolerate pain better than men? Why?

Partner 1 ____________________

Partner 2 ____________________

Q5. What kind of pain are you most afraid of?

Partner 1 ______________________________

Partner 2 ______________________________

Q6. ______________________________? (Make your own question)

Partner 1 ______________________________

Partner 2 ______________________________

Q7. ______________________________? (Make your own question)

Partner 1 ______________________________

Partner 2 ______________________________

Q8. ______________________________? (Make your own question)

Partner 1 ______________________________

Partner 2 ______________________________

5 Dialogue

Listen to Nurse Tanaka talking to James, an 11-year old boy.

Nurse Tanaka: What seems to be the problem, little boy?

James: I broke my arm when I was playing outside. I fell off my bicycle and landed on my arms. I heard a cracking sound!

Nurse Tanaka: Oh dear! Let's have a look at that. It does look swollen. On a scale from 1 to 10, how bad is the pain?

James: About 8 or 9. I can't move my arm also.

Nurse Tanaka: You need an X-ray.

James: Will I be able to use my arm again?

Nurse Tanaka: Let's ask the doctor. He is the expert.

Role play Exercises

1. Practice the dialogue with a partner.
2. Practice the dialogue again. This time talk about pain in another body part.

6 Voice message: A message left in Tom's answering service of his mobile phone

George: Hey dude! What's up? I haven't heard from you in a long time. How's Japan? I hope you're having a blast over there!

George: Hey Tom. Did you get my message yesterday? I hope you weren't kid-napped by ninjas! Give me a buzz ok?

George: Tom. George again. I'm starting to get worried. You haven't replied in 3 days. This is unlike you. Are you ok over there?

George: Dude, sorry to hear about the accident. I heard about it from your Mom. Take care man and get well soon! I hope to see you in great shape again when I visit Japan next month. Meanwhile, wish me luck with my finals at UCLA!

Questions

1. Who is George?
2. Was Tom kidnapped by ninjas?
3. What does the expression "This is unlike you" mean?
4. Is George a student? How did you know?

7 Quiz

Rearrange the letters to reveal a word that means pain in a certain part of the body.

1. CHEEARA E ______________
2. AASOMTCHCHE S ______________
3. CTOTOHAHE T ______________
4. ABCCKEHA B ______________
5. EAHAHCED H ______________
6. ROSE RHOATT S ________ T ________
7. STCHE PINA C ________ P ________
8. CLEMUS AIPN M ________ P ________
9. FFITS CENK S ________ N ________
10. CHETHAREA H ______________

8 Reading comprehension

Experience in medical care in Japan.

Gall bladder surgery

I had severe pain in my abdomen for a week. I lost my appetite and could not sleep at night. I did not think it was anything serious, but when I went to the hospital for a checkup, my blood test revealed everything was abnormal. I had gallstones. The doctor arranged for immediate surgery in the afternoon. I asked if I can postpone the surgery for another three days because of work, but the doctor warned me that I may not live if I wait that long. I was shocked to hear that and prepared for surgery without delay.

The doctors inserted a tube in my bile duct to facilitate the flow of bile and avoid damage to my pancreas. My blood was checked every day to see if the numbers would return to normal level. After a week of IV drip only, my blood test result slowly returned to normal. And in order to avoid a recurrence, the doctor advised me to undergo *laparascopic cholecystectomy* (surgical removal of the gall bladder).

The surgery lasted about two hours. I was under general anesthesia and everything went smoothly. I was told to immediately start walking the next day for a speedy recovery. After staying in the hospital for a couple more days, I was allowed to go home.

Answer the following questions about the text:

1. What kind of pain was the author suffering from?
2. Why was it not possible to delay the surgery?
3. How long did the surgery last?
4. In order to have a speedy recovery, what did the author do?

Chapter 5

Operation, body organs

1 Useful Vocabulary

- general anesthesia
- next of kin
- surgery
- local anesthesia
- health insurance

② Useful expressions

Common expressions to find out if the other person can meet you next time are: *Are you free?* Or *Are you available?*

This is often followed by the kind of activity (e.g. meeting, date, interview) and the day of the week (e.g. Monday, tomorrow).

For example: *Are you free/available for a check-up tomorrow/next week/on Monday?*

The answer would be: *Yes, I am.* Or *No, I'm not.*

If the answer is "No, I'm not", a common follow-up question would be:

How about tomorrow/next week?

This expression seeks to find another time when the speakers can meet.

The reply would then be: *Yes, I am free / available. / No, I'm not. Sorry.*

Another common question is: *When are you free / available?*
This expression is used when the other person continues to say he or she is not available.

The other person would now reply with: *I am free/available tomorrow/next week/on Monday.*

In order to find out if the patient has health insurance, ask the question:

Do you have health insurance?

The answer would either be: *Yes, I do.* Or *No, I don't.*

To find out who is the closest relative to the patient, ask this question:

Who is your next of kin?

The patient would then reply with: *My mother / father / brother / sister.*

Useful expressions practice

1. Are you __________ for a blood test tomorrow? Yes, _______. / No, _______.
2. When are you __________ ? I am available __________ .
3. Do you have health insurance __________? Yes, ______ / No, ______.
4. Who is your next of kin? __________.

3 Listening

Nurse Tanaka and Nurse Sato study English, so they tend to practice their English together and with Ann.

Listen to the following interview and fill in the blanks with the missing words. Practice the dialogue with a partner.

Nurse Tanaka: Have you ever donated blood, Ann?

Ann: No, I haven't. This is my first time and frankly, I am a bit __________.

Nurse Tanaka: Don't worry. It's a simple procedure. You'll be fine. Now, please extend your arm.

Ann: Which arm?

Nurse Tanaka: Are you right-handed or left-handed?

Ann: Left-handed.

Nurse Tanaka: Let's see. Why don't we use your right arm?

Ann: OK.

Nurse Tanaka: Now, please clench your __________ while I tie a tourniquet around your arm.

Ann: Like this?

Nurse: Yes. I'll just rub some __________ on your arm before sticking a needle. You will feel a small pin prick.

Ann: Ouch!

Nurse Tanaka: You can relax your hand now. It will be over soon.... Alright. That's it. I have collected __________ of blood from you. Now, press this gauze pad on your arm for about 5 minutes.

Ann: Thank goodness it's over. But now that I have __________ blood, I realized it's not that painful. I was scared for nothing.

Nurse Tanaka: Good to hear you say that. So, shall we schedule your next blood donation after 6 months ?

Ann: Uh... let me think about that.

4 Pair work

Interview 2 classmates and write their answers.

Q1. Do you have any allergies?

Partner 1 ______________________________

Partner 2 ______________________________

Q2. Do you eat a lot of meat?

Partner 1 ______________________________

Partner 2 ______________________________

Q3. What kinds of food do you like?

Partner 1 ______________________________

Partner 2 ______________________________

Q4. Do you eat a lot of sweets?

Partner 1 ______________________________

Partner 2 ______________________________

Q5. Do you take any supplements?

Partner 1 ______________________________

Partner 2 ______________________________

Q6. ______________________________? (Make your own question)

Partner 1 ______________________________

Partner 2 ______________________________

Q7. ______________________________? (Make your own question)

Partner 1 ______________________________

Partner 2 ______________________________

Q8. ______________________________? (Make your own question)

Partner 1 ______________________________

Partner 2 ______________________________

1. Have you experienced any surgical procedure before?
2. What kind of surgery are you most afraid of?
3. If you have a choice, would you prefer general or local anesthesia?

4. Would you undergo surgery for cosmetic reasons (in order to look more attractive)?
5. Have you ever donated blood?

5 Dialogue

Nurse Tanaka and Nurse Sato are practicing their English.

Nurse Tanaka: Nurse Sato, are you available for work on Saturday?
Nurse Sato: This coming Saturday?
Tanaka: Yes, I need to take my mother to an ophthalmologist for cataract surgery. I was wondering if you can fill in for me?
Sato: No problem. I don't have anything to do this weekend.
Tanaka: Oh, thank you very much. I owe you another one.
Sato: Don't be silly. You always fill in for me whenever I can't come for work.
Tanaka: I really appreciate your help. Thanks again.
Sato: You're very much welcome. I wish your mom the best with her surgery

Role-play practice

1. Practice the dialogue with a partner.
2. Practice the dialogue again. This time you are not available.

6 Telephone conversation between Tom and George

Tom finally answered his friend, George's call before his operation.
Read the following telephone conversation and answer the questions.

Tom: Hey George! It's Tom. Sorry for the long silence. Yeah, I'm in a hospital here in Japan and scheduled for surgery tomorrow.
George: Is everything OK?
Tom: Yes, the doctors and nurses are really looking after me. Everyone is so kind and I feel everything's going to be fine with my leg.
George: It's compartment syndrome, isn't it? Never heard of it before.
Tom: Me neither. I heard in extreme cases, the limb gets amputated!
George: Oh man! That's so uncool! I hope you get well-soon!

Tom: Thanks, buddy. I look forward to seeing you again soon. Break a leg with the finals!

George: Don't say that! I don't want to break any leg. Hahaha...

Tom: Hahaha... yeah, I shouldn't wish that for anyone. Anyway, I hope you ace the finals like you always do!

George: Thanks dude. See you real soon! By the way, a little birdie told me about a certain Ann. Who is she?

Tom: Uh... that's a long story.

George: Uh-huh? Is she.... ?

Tom: No, no... she's just a friend.

George: Well, if you say so. Now, I really need to get there as soon as I can.... Anyway, all the best with the surgery!

Tom: Thanks. Catch you later, old chum!

Questions

1. Will Tom's leg get amputated?
2. What does the expression "break a leg" mean?
3. What does the expression "ace the finals" mean?
4. What did George want to ask about Ann?

7 Quiz

Rearrange the letters to reveal an internal organ.

1. TAHER	H ____________
2. GNUL	L ____________
3. YINDEK	K ____________
4. SPANCEAR	P ____________
5. VLIRE	L ____________
6. ALGL REDLABD	G ______ B ______
7. CHASOMT	S ____________
8. GREAL ININTTEES	L ______ I ______
9. LAMLS EINSTTEIN	S ______ I ______
10. ENSPEL	S ____________

8 Reading comprehension

DID YOU KNOW?

The 1st nursing school was established in India in 250 B.C.

During this time, only men were allowed to attend the school because they were viewed as more pure than women. Now woman practically dominate the field statistically. Data from the 2009 U.S Department of Health and Human Services stated that approximately 5.8% of nurses in the U.S were male. It wasn't until the 1800's that nursing truly became a systematized practice.

Nurses walk on average 4 miles (6.4 km) a day

A MEDSURG Nursing study called "How Far Do Nurses Walk?" found that 146 nurses walked an average of 4-5 miles (6.4 -8.0 km) total during their 12-hour shift. Compare that to the average American, who only walks 2.5-3 miles on average daily. It's no surprise that nurses manage to get those steps in. They're on their feet for 12 hours straight!

(Save a Life by NHCPS (2020). 10 Facts About Nursing. Retrieved [2020.3.24] with permission from https://nhcps.com/you-should-know-these-ten-remarkable-facts-about-nursing/)

Answer the following questions about the text:

1. In the past, why were women not allowed to become nurses?
2. Do you think male nurses are better than female nurses?
3. How far do nurses walk compared to the average American?
4. Were you surprised about how far nurses walk?

Chapter 6

Post-operative care and administration of hospitalization

1 Useful Vocabulary

- ROM
- antibiotics
- post-op
- strenuous

2 Useful expressions

Should: modal verb used in making recommendations or giving advice

Positive: You **should** take your medications as prescribed.

Negative: You **should not** smoke after the surgery.

Ought to: a little stronger than **should** (a kind of judgment)
Had better: much stronger than **should** (a kind of warning)

You **ought to** take your medications as prescribed.

You **had better** not smoke after the surgery.

Have to, Need to, Must: model verbs expressing necessity. Americans usually use **have to** instead of **must**.

You **have to** undergo rehabilitation exercises.

You **need to** eat healthy food.

You **must** contact your doctor if you are experiencing unbearable pain.

Practice: Make a list of Do's and Don'ts after undergoing surgery.

3 Listening

Nurse Tanaka and Nurse Sato study English, so they tend to practice their English together and with Ann.
Listen to the following interview and fill in the blanks with the missing words. Practice the dialogue with a partner.

Ann: Thank you for taking good care of Tom.
Nurse Sato: Not at all. We're just doing our job.
Ann: Still we are grateful for all you are doing to make sure Tom's surgery goes well.
Nurse Sato: Well, now that the surgery is finished, we need to focus on post-op ____________.
Ann: What is going to happen next?
Nurse Sato: As part of the rehabilitation process, there will be passive and active ROM ____________.
Ann: ROM?

Nurse Sato: ROM means Range of Motion. Passive ROM refers to exercises where the patient does not need to exert any _________. Active ROM means the patient needs to move using his own muscles.

Ann: I see. I hope the exercises are not too _________ for Tom.

Nurse Sato: Don't worry. The therapist will closely monitor his _________ strength and flexibility.

4 Pair work

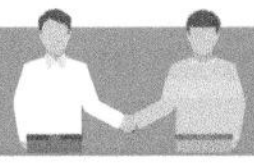

Interview 2 classmates and write their answers.

Q1. Do you know anyone who underwent surgery?

Partner 1 ____

Partner 2 ____

Q2. What would be difficult to do after surgery?

Partner 1 ____

Partner 2 ____

Q3. Would you donate your organ (kidney or liver) to a relative?

Partner 1 ____

Partner 2 ____

Q4. Would you donate your organ (kidney or liver) to a friend?

Partner 1 ____

Partner 2 ____

Q5. What was the longest time that you have been hospitalized?

Partner 1 ____

Partner 2 ____

Q6. __________________________________? (Make your own question)

Partner 1 ____

Partner 2 ____

Q7. __________________________________? (Make your own question)

Partner 1 ____

Partner 2 ____

Q8. __________________________________? (Make your own question)

Partner 1 ____

Partner 2 ____

5 Dialogue

Listen to Nurse Tanaka talking to Tom after the operation.

Nurse Tanaka: Tom, here is a list of things you should do and things you should not do. Please read it carefully.

Tom: Thanks. Uh-oh, it says I should not drive a car.

Nurse Tanaka: Yes, it's only temporary until you get a lot better. In the meantime, you could call a taxi or ask a friend or family member to drive you home.

Tom: I understand.

Nurse Tanaka: Be careful also not to stop taking antibiotics even if you are feeling a bit better. Stopping antibiotics too early might increase the risk of antibiotic resistance.

Tom: Oh, I did not know that. Thanks. I'll not forget to take my full course of antibiotics.

Nurse Tanaka: Good. And if you follow everything on this list, you are on your way to a speedy recovery.

Exercises

1. Practice the dialogue with a partner.
2. Practice the dialogue again. This time talk about other post-operation do's and don'ts.

6 Text message: Ann text to her mother

Ann: Mom, Tom's operation went well.

Mother: Good. When can he go home?

Ann: Probably after a week. He needs to stay at the hospital for observation.

Mother: I see. I hope he can have a speedy recovery.

Ann: Me too. His parents there in the UK must be really worried about him.

Mother: I know. They're even considering flying out to see Tom in person.

Ann: Tell them not to worry. The doctors and nurses assure Tom that the surgery went well.

Questions

1. Where is Ann's mother?
2. When can Tom go home?
3. Does Ann's mom know Tom's parents?
4. Will Tom's parents visit him in Japan?

7 Vocabulary Puzzle

Look for the following medical conditions.

1. Cancer
2. Diabetes
3. Stroke
4. Pneumonia
5. Ulcer
6. Tuberculosis
7. Appendicitis
8. Hypertension
9. Hepatitis
10. Heart Attack
11. Asthma
12. Dementia
13. Arthritis
14. Epilepsy
15. Glaucoma

C	E	S	P	C	A	N	C	E	R	O	L	N	T	I	S	A	D	A	N
A	D	A	V	H	S	W	R	N	O	N	E	O	A	N	T	D	E	P	Y
N	I	R	M	A	I	T	U	B	E	R	C	U	L	O	S	I	S	P	O
D	A	T	E	P	C	A	G	B	R	H	E	T	L	Y	A	T	M	E	R
A	B	A	R	N	I	S	H	Y	P	E	R	T	E	N	S	I	O	N	O
C	E	R	T	E	B	W	E	D	N	A	O	I	N	G	H	N	A	D	E
K	T	A	M	U	G	U	L	C	E	R	O	P	M	Q	Z	E	M	I	J
E	E	F	I	M	S	T	O	O	Q	T	N	B	T	H	A	S	T	C	Y
P	S	T	R	O	K	E	S	W	H	A	D	T	R	O	H	A	G	I	N
I	D	U	B	N	I	M	O	A	R	T	S	Y	I	N	E	Z	H	T	A
L	E	X	Y	I	D	A	M	S	E	T	T	A	M	B	P	Y	G	I	P
E	Y	U	B	A	R	O	H	M	Q	A	S	T	H	M	A	R	H	S	O
P	H	O	T	I	C	X	W	U	U	C	A	U	W	C	T	O	N	L	W
S	U	M	E	U	Q	U	I	G	A	K	I	B	J	A	I	F	A	Y	D
Y	M	P	A	S	T	Y	Y	O	V	W	P	X	H	D	T	R	I	P	M
T	E	L	D	E	I	R	M	N	D	E	M	E	N	T	I	A	D	U	N
R	G	A	S	E	N	T	A	R	T	H	R	I	T	I	S	Y	R	E	G

8 Extra Reading

SKI ACCIDENT

I was just learning to ski when I went to Meiho Ski Resort in Gifu with a friend who can ski very well. After a few successful rounds on the lower slopes, my friend suggested we try going to the top of the mountain. We did and that was a very big mistake for me. When I tried to imitate my friend's skiing style, I lost my balance and both legs went to opposite directions. I could not stop until finally I heard something popped. I twisted my knee and could not stand up, so the emergency crew took me down the mountain on a sled.

I went to a big hospital in Nagoya and the young doctor who examined my leg for five minutes declared that I should just go home and rest. He said the X-ray did not reveal any broken bones.

I was not satisfied with the young doctor's assessment, so I went to another hospital specializing in orthopedics. Aside from X-ray, I had an MRI scan and that was when it became clear that my MCL[1] was partially torn. There was no need for me to undergo surgery, but I had to wear a mechanical brace for three months. I also had to undergo physical therapy every week.

[1]MCL (medial collateral ligament) —It is the tissue that connects the bottom of the thigh bone with the top of the shinbone. It helps stabilize the knee.

Answer the following questions about the text:

1. Why was it a big mistake to go to the top of the mountain?
2. Why did he go to another hospital?
3. What was wrong with his leg?
4. Do you think he will ski again?

Chapter 7

Taking Medicine

1 Useful Vocabulary

- wound
- antiseptic
- antibiotics
- anti-inflammatory
- surgical tape
- surgical gloves
- always
- bandage
- IV
- painkillers
- syringe
- surgical scissors
- gauze
- usually

- often
- sometimes
- occasionally
- hardly ever
- never

2 Grammar Focus

How often	do I / you / we / they does he / she	take this medication? change the bandage? the doctor do rounds?

I You He /She We They	always usually often sometimes occasionally hardly ever never	have / have medication in an IV. change / changes the bandage. discharge / discharges the patient after day surgery.

once twice three times	a (an) / every	_____hours(s) _____day(s) _____week(s) etc.

3 Listening

Changing a bandage.

Listen to the conversation and answer the questions that follow.

Nurse A: The surgical gloves are on the top shelf. We each need a pair.

Student Nurse B: Certainly, here you are.

Nurse A: Thanks. Now can you pass me the surgical scissors? They are on the middle shelf.

Student Nurse B: Of course. Do we need anything else?

Nurse A: Yes. We'll need a syringe, saline, some gauze and fresh bandages.

Student Nurse B: Oh...mmm...I'm sorry. Where can I find them?

Nurse A: The syringes are next to the scissors on the middles shelf, the saline is beside the gloves on the top shelf, and the gauze is between the surgical tape and bandages on the bottom shelf.

Questions

1. Where are the scissors?
2. What shelf is the saline on?
3. What is next to the surgical gloves?
4. What is in the bottom drawer?
5. What is to the left of the scissors?

4 Pair work

Draw two sets of three shelves on your paper. Take turns with your partner to

a) Place the items from the listening exercise on the shelves and ask your partner where they are.

b) Put them in different places, tell your partner where they are and have your partner listen and write them in the correct place.

5 Writing

Tom texts his mother to update his family about his medication and the plan for his rehabilitation. Write 4 or 5 sentences.

6 Quiz

Get into two teams. Read the clues and find the answers in the text. Write them on a paper.

What 's' are gloves that medical staff use?
What 'a' means everyday?
What 's' is salty water?
What 'a' is medicine used for or to prevent infections?
What 'g' is placed on top of a cut under the bandage?

7 Reading comprehension

Experiences in medical care in Japan or abroad or related trivia.

Medical English has a lot of different forms, not only between British and American English, but also between medical staff and patients. Surgeons talk about “incisions” during operations but many patients understand these as ‘wounds’. Doctors prescribe their patients with “analgesics” which patients refer to as “painkillers”. “Sutures” is the medical term for “stitches” which are used to close incisions (wounds) after operations. An IV, which is American English, is the abbreviation of intravenous drip, but British people call this a drip... Confusing, right??

Questions

1. Who says “sutures”?
2. What’s the everyday term for “analgesic”?
3. What’s the medical term for a “drip”?
4. What’s another word for an “incision”?
5. When do we need “stitches”?

Chapter 8

Nutrition and Allergies

1 Useful Vocabulary

- recovery
- avoid
- alcohol
- salt
- vitamin D
- calories
- possibility
- nutrients
- caffeine
- sugar
- calcium
- vitamin C
- protein
- for sure

- probably
- maybe
- impossible
- perhaps
- probably not

2 Useful expressions ‘Possibility (will, won’t)’

Will

Rapid Decision

I’m hungry. I think I **will** buy a hamburger.

Offer

That looks heavy. I **will** help you with it.

Promise

Don’t worry, I **won’t** forget to call.

Threat

If you don’t stop, I **will** send you to the principal’s office.

Refusal (won’t = will not)

She **won’t** listen to anything I say.

Write a sentence for each of the above.
Share your sentences with a partner and then act out the sentences.

1. Rapid decision
2. Offer
3. Promise
4. Threat
5. Refusal

3 Listening

Listen to the dialogue between Tom and the nutritionist. Answer the questions below. Then compare your answer to your partner’s.

Nutritionist(Ann translated): Tom, let’s talk about your diet. Recovery speed and effectiveness after orthopaedic surgery are helped by what we eat.

Tom: Okay, so what food will help me recover quicker?

Nutritionist: Well, let's first talk about the 4 important nutrients. Protein, vitamin C, calcium and vitamin D.

Tom: Protein. So I'll need to eat a lot of meat?

Nutritionist: Protein can also be found in soy, dairy, beans, eggs, chicken, fish, meat and nuts.

Tom: Hmmm. I'm allergic to nuts and I'm a vegetarian so it sounds like it will be difficult.

Nutritionist: You should also avoid caffeine, alcohol, excessive sugar and salt. They slow down bone healing.

Exercise

Answer the questions below.

1. What helps with recovery speed?
2. What are the 4 important nutrients?
3. Name 3 foods that are high in protein.
4. What is Tom allergic to?
5. What should Tom avoid and why?

4 Pair work

Read the questions below. Make up three of your own questions.
Interview 2 classmates. 'Answer more' for each question. Write your partners answers.

Q1. Do you have any allergies?

Partner 1 ______________________________

Partner 2 ______________________________

Q2. Do you eat a lot of meat?

Partner 1 ______________________________

Partner 2 ______________________________

Q3. What foods do you like?

Partner 1 ______________________________

Partner 2 ______________________________

Q4. Do you eat a lot of sugar?

Partner 1 ______________________________

Partner 2 ______________________________

Q5. Do you take any supplements?

Partner 1 ____________________

Partner 2 ____________________

Write your own questions for 6-8.

Q6. ____________________?

Partner 1 ____________________

Partner 2 ____________________

Q7. ____________________?

Partner 1 ____________________

Partner 2 ____________________

Q8. ____________________?

Partner 1 ____________________

Partner 2 ____________________

5 Blog

Here I am in my new 'home'. I'll probably be here for a week. I'm going to be so bored. On the up side, I'll have lots of time to write my blog. That's good. I promise I'll post every day and let you know how my recovery is going. I probably won't upload many photos. These white walls aren't very interesting. I won't make you look at them, even though I have to. Hmm, maybe I'll go outside for some fresh air... Yes! I've decided. I'll go outside after I finish writing this blog post. I won't be walking on my leg. I'm still on crutches.

So, what should I do with all this free time? Leave suggestions in the comment. I promise I'll answer you.

Exercise

In groups talk about some suggestions for what Tom can do in his free time? Try using the language you learned in chapter 6 (should, could.)

6 About the Future

Rank

1. For sure it will happen.
2. It’ll probably happen in the next few years.
3. Maybe it’ll happen.
4. It probably won’t happen
5. It’ll never happen.

Future Possibility -will					
Possible event	Rank (circle one)				
People will live on Mars.	1	2	3	4	5
A chip for languages will be put in the brain. You won’t have to study English!	1	2	3	4	5
Nurses will be replaced with robots.	1	2	3	4	5
People will live for 200 years.	1	2	3	4	5
All people will become vegetarian.	1	2	3	4	5
Surgery will become obsolete. Stem cell therapy will be used instead.	1	2	3	4	5

Exercise

Will the events above be good or bad for the world? Discuss in groups.

If you have finished your work, try reading the following. Discuss in small groups.

7 Extra Reading

I used to have a pet monkey. It was a Squirrel Monkey. He came to live with me when his previous owner suddenly left. There was no one to take care of Monta. At first I was okay but, little by little I started to have various symptoms. I got a lot of ear infections. I had a persistent cough. I caught colds easily. Finally, I got a bad rash that spread from my face, to my neck, to my arms. I went to see a dermatologist and she tested me for allergies. I had become allergic to everything around me. Even Aloe Vera! I found out that it was all caused by my first allergy to my pet monkey. I had to find him a new place to live. Luckily I found him a home with another Squirrel monkey.

All my symptoms disappeared after that. Recently, I got a pet cat. I hope the rash, the earaches and the cough don't come back again.

Chapter 9

Maternity Outpatient

A British pregnant woman comes for a check-up with her husband.

1 Useful Vocabulary

- DPO (days past ovulation)
- anti-natal
- EDD (estimated date of delivery)
- post partum
- trimester
- birth
- ultrasound
- craving
- premature
- non stress test
- incubator
- morning sickness
- c-section
- monitor

- delivery
- conception
- induction
- epidural / spinal block
- birth-plan
- skin-to-skin

2 Useful Expressions

'Modal verbs, may, might, could happen, expressing possibility'

I	may/ might/ could	have pre-eclampsia
You		be in labour
She		need a c-section
It		be a sign of placenta previa
We		be in the wrong position
They		
The doctor		
The baby		

3 Listening

Listen to the following interview and answer the questions that follow. Then compare your answer to your partner's.

Midwife: Mrs. Ash is it ok if I ask you some questions?

Mrs. Ash: Of course.

Midwife: Is this your first pregnancy?

Mrs. Ash: No, we have a 2 year old daughter.

Midwife: Was she full term? Were there any complications with the birth?

Mrs. Ash: She was born by c-section at 41 weeks.

Midwife: Why was that?

Mrs. Ash: It was a failed induction.

Midwife: How many weeks pregnant are you now?

Mrs. Ash: I'm 16 weeks and 2 days.

Midwife: The second trimester then. Any symptoms or problems?

Mrs. Ash: Well I have morning sickness and often feel dizzy. I'm also craving cheese.

Midwife: Try not to eat too much!

Question

1. Is this Mrs. Ash's first baby?
2. When did she have the c-section?
3. How many weeks pregnant is she?
4. When is her EDD?
5. What are her symptoms?

4 Pair work

Practice the conversation above with a partner with the following information:

Mrs Black	Mrs Jones	Mrs Smith
4 year old son	6 year old twins	9 month old daughter
inducton at 34 weeks	c-section at 36 weeks	induction at 42 weeks
baby wasn't growing	multiple delivery	didn't go into labour
8 weeks 5 days	32 weeks 4 days	12 weeks 1 day
1st trimester	3rd trimester	2nd trimester

5 Short Writing Exercise

Ann receives the following text from her friend who is a student midwife. Reply to it in 4 sentences.

Hi Ann! A really nice British lady came to our hospital today. She was very surprised that she can't use her health insurance for maternity visits. I tried to explain that usually pregnancy isn't an illness in Japan. Do you think she understood?

6 Quiz

In teams listen to the information and try to calculate the possible date of conception or due date. The closest date wins.

Date of Conception	Due Date
March 6	(　　　　　)
(　　　　　)	June 5
January 30	(　　　　　)
(　　　　　)	December 30
July 3	(　　　　　)
(　　　　　)	November 7
October 11	(　　　　　)
(　　　　　)	May 4

*the due date is calculated by adding 280 days to the first day of the last menstrual period.

7 Extra Reading

Experiences in medical care in Japan or abroad or related trivia.

Japan and the UK have a few surprising differences when it comes to pregnancy and birth. One difference is that Japanese women talk about being pregnant for ten months while in Britain, its nine. The forty weeks recognized as the typical length of a normal pregnancy is actually half way between nine and ten months!

Another difference is that having a ‘birthing partner’ present for the delivery (including elective c-sections) in Britain is much more common in Britain than in Japan and British women can have pain relief in the form of pethidine, morphine, etonox (nitrous oxide) or an epidural/spinal block while in Japan, natural childbirth without pain relief is much more frequent.

Question

1. In which country is the use of pain relief during childbirth more common?
2. How many months is considered a ‘full term’ pregnancy in Japan?
3. What’s the name of a person who supports a pregnant woman during childbirth?
4. What kinds of pain relief are available in the UK during labour?
5. Where is natural birth free of pain relief more common?

Chapter 10

Pediatric Outpatient

Ann translates for the Scottish girl and her mother using children's English.

1 Useful Vocabulary

- vomiting
- flinch
- cough
- fever
- torso
- limbs
- tuberculosis
- stickers
- mumps
- diarrhea
- clench
- rash
- tongue
- measles
- immunization
- needle

2 Useful expressions

'Imperative, Likes & Dislikes'

Breathe in! Touch your toes!

Open your mouth wide! Follow my pen with your eyes!

Don't flinch! Don't clench your arm!

Don't be afraid. Don't cry.

(*with adults add please to give instructions more formally eg. Touch your toes please...Please don't worry.)

Do you / we / they like gummy bears?

Does he / she like stickers?

cute erasers?

Yes, I / you / he / she / we / they do / does.

No, I / you / he / she / we / they don't / doesn't

What do you / they like? I / we / they like ___________.

What does he / she like? He / she likes ______________.

3 Dialogue / Listening

Ann: Hello there! Are you buying snacks too?

Meg's mother: Meg's getting a treat because she was brave.

Ann: Well done! I'm not good at being brave. I don't like needles.

Meg: I got two stickers - one for a blood draw and one for the big needle with the medicine.

Meg's mother: She has a fever and a stomachache so she needed an IV and a blood test.

Ann: If you try to drink enough you'll get better soon.

Meg: I'll do my best!

Questions

1. What did Ann buy at the convenience store?
2. What do neither Ann nor Meg Like?
3. What did Meg get the two stickers for?
4. What's wrong with Meg?
5. What did Ann say Meg should try to do?

④ Pair work

Ask your partner about their immunization record. Compare it with your own immunization record.

Immunization	Yes / No	When?
Were you immunized for polio?		
tuberculosis?		
tetanus?		
diphtheria?		
whooping cough?		
mumps?		
measles?		
rubella?		
Japanese (B) encephalitis?		
chicken pox?		
influenza ?		

⑤ Short Writing Exercise

Write a text message to your friend telling him/ her about an illness you had as a child. Write five sentences.

⑥ Quiz

a) In pairs, take turns giving each other instructions and miming them while ignoring those which begin with “Don’t”.
b) In pairs take turns miming and interpreting instructions.

7 Extra Reading

Many illnesses have Latin names which are usually used only by doctors and more common names which are used by everybody else. Two examples of this is "varicella" which is more commonly known as chickenpox and "pertussis" which is usually called "whooping cough." One of these childhood illnesses, Roseola Infantum, doesn't have a common name in British English because it is very rarely diagnosed. This illness, which is neither serious nor life threatening, is very often diagnosed in Japan in babies who are one year old or less. One reason for this could be that British mothers do not tend to seek help when a low grade fever is the only symptom and the condition disappears within 48 hours of contracting it. The symptoms of Roseola Infantum are a fever for around 48 hours which disappears when a non-itchy red rash appears on the torso and limbs.

Questions

1. What's the common name for varicella?
2. What's the medical name for whooping cough?
3. Why is Roseola Infantum less diagnosed in Britain than in Japan?
4. How long does Rosela Infantum last?
5. What are the symptoms of Roseola Infantum?

Chapter 11

Out of Hospital (Looking back at his time there)

1 Useful Vocabulary 1

- discharge
- South East Asia

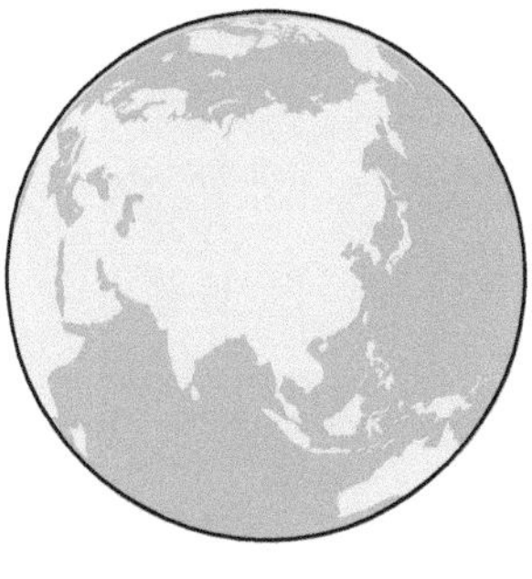

② Useful expressions 1

You have been discharged.
You have been hospitalized.
He has been dismissed.
You have been framed!

What are you up to? What are you doing?

I would love to come. (Strong liking)
I want to come. (Strong desire to have)
I would like to come.(Firm preference)

③ Role-play practice

Tom retrospectively remembers his conversation with Nutritionist.

Nutritionist(Ann translated): You can't have any salty food for a few weeks.
Tom: Why not?
Nutritionist: The doctor is worried about your kidney function. and the hospital meals are mostly Japanese dishes. Can you use chopsticks Tom?
Tom: Not very well, a knife and fork would be better.
Tom: Can I have my friend bring me some soda and coffee when he visits?
Nutritionist: It's probably not a good idea to drink these while you're on strong medication.

4 Useful Vocabulary 2

Be allowed to ________.

Be on medication (for ________).

Request.

Permission

Will you let me ________? May I ________?

Could you ________?

Crutches

Bed rest

Nurse call button

5 Useful expressions 2

'Can/could/May for permission/request'

1. Can I have a bath today?
2. You can't get out of bed yet, you're only 6 hours post op.
3. May I take your blood pressure and temperature please?
4. Could you ask the doctor if I can start to walk tomorrow?
5. You won't be allowed to go home until you can walk up and downstairs by yourself.

6 Listening

Listen to the following passage and answer the questions that follow.

Hospital rules are different from country to country and even hospitals in the same country sometimes have different rules.

Rules for visiting sick patients are quite strict. There are usually two times in a day when a patient can have visitors - in the afternoon for about an hour, and in the evening for about an hour. This of course depends on the stage of treatment, type of illness and condition of the patient's health.

The maximum number of visitors per patient is two at the one time and parents are usually requested not to bring young children to visit a sick patient. Hospitals also prefer people not to visit if they have been in contact with anyone who has a cold or flu symptoms and will provide a phone number for family members to call for an update on the patient's health instead.

Questions

1. When can a patient usually have visitors?
2. Which three factors determine if a patient can have visitors?
3. How many visitors can a patient have at a time?
4. Who should not visit a sick patient?
5. When shouldn't you visit a sick patient? What should you do instead?

Complete the following questions for permission and request.

May I ________? (permission)

Could I ________? (permission)

Can I ________? (permission)

Would you __________ please? (request)

Could you __________ please? (request)

Can you ____________ please? (request)

Interview 2 classmates and write their answers.

7 Dialogue

Read the conversation and circle the answer.

Doctor: Do you have any questions?

Tom: When will I be able to have visitors?

Doctor: Not for the next 24 hours. If your temperature is normal tomorrow morning, you can have one visitor tomorrow evening.

Tom: I'm pretty hungry, can I have lunch?

Doctor: It's best to stick to water until the anaesthetic wears off. You'll be able to eat a light meal for breakfast.

Tom: Will I be able to have a shower tomorrow?

Doctor: You can't get out of bed for the next 2 or 3 days until your incision heals. The nursing staff will help you with bed baths until then. If all goes well, you can have a shower on Tuesday.

Tom: Ok, thanks.

Questions

Circle the correct choose.

1. Hopefully Tom can have a visitor tomorrow morning/tomorrow evening.
2. Tom can have a visitor/visitors.
3. Tom can have a light meal for breakfast/lunch.
4. Tom must stay in bed for the next 24 days/2 or 3 days.
5. Tom wants to have a bath/shower on Tuesday/Thursday.

8 Tom's Blog 'A day in the hospital'

I'm going to describe my hospital room. I'm sharing a room with three other men who have all had surgery on their legs. My bed is next to the window which overlooks the car park. We each have a bedside table and a small locker to keep our valuables in and a curtain pulls round our bed to give us privacy at night. There's a socket on the wall behind my head where I can charge my mobile phone and I have a reading lamp also. The bathroom and toilets are directly across from our room so we don't have to go far!

Exercise

Draw a simple picture of Tom's hospital room from the description in his blog.

9 Game

In a circle or in groups of four people ask and answer questions with can/could/may? Only questions of permission or request should be answered and questions about ability should be ignored. Anyone who answers the wrong question loses and the last student wins.

10 Extra Reading

I've been treated in hospital five times in the 30 years. I've been in Japan and each time I've experienced some aspects of medical care which were different from my own country. Of all of these experiences the most surprising (for me) was connected to bathtime!

I was in hospital for two weeks being treated for pleural pneumonia and in the second week I felt well enough to have a shower. For about ten days I couldn't do more than wash with hot towels so I was really looking forward to washing my hair!

I asked another patient where the showers were and went there after I told a nurse (in English) that I was going for a wash. About ten minutes later the nurse in charge of the ward that day rushed into the bathroom in a panic and began to tell me in a loud voice that I needed to get back to bed straight away. She seemed angry so I was very confused until a doctor later explained to me that patients in Japan do not usually take a bath or a shower in case it makes them sick. I told him I thought it was crazy to think that being dirty was better for my health and he was very surprised to learn that in other countries it's quite normal to have showers during treatment if the patient feels well enough to wash him/herself.

Chapter 12

Palliative Care

Ann was called to Palliative care unit because a patient who was born and raised in US needed to talk in English.

1 Useful Vocabulary

- volunteer
- palliative care
- cousin
- nephew and niece
- translator
- grandparents and grandchild
- uncle and aunt
- hospice

2 Useful expressions

'simple past, Wh-questions, expressing desire, conditional, which prefer, request, regret'

Now I go to school by bus.
But I used to go to school by bicycle when I was a junior school student.

Present habit(custom)
Past habit(custom)

Used	To
Did	Use to?

I used to go to school by bicycle.
Did you use to be very active when you were a child?

What would you like to do if had a lot of money?

Would	Like	To /(noun)
Would	Love	To /(noun)
Would	Prefer	~ing /(noun)

I wish I didn't.
I wish I could.
I wish I hadn't done that.
I wished you hadn't said that.

3 Listening

Listen to the following interview and circle the answer you hear.
Then compare your answer to your partner's.

Mike: Hi, which high school did you go to?

Jim: Well, I went to Folkstone grammar school. A grammar school is like a high school.

Mike: I see. Was it a single sex school or coeducational?

Jim: It was boys only. They wanted keep us away from the girls.

Mike: Oh really? How many students were there?

Jim: About 700 pupils, aged 11 to 18.

Mike: What is your best memory from school?

Jim: Leaving it! Hahahaha. I suppose lunch time with friends was the best.

Mike: I bet. How did you get there?

Jim: By double decker bus, always on the top deck.

Mike: What sort of sports activities did you do at school?

Jim: I tried to avoid sports I'm afraid, but in summer we did athletics and played cricket. Hockey and Football in winter, and cross country running when the ground was too wet for the other sports.

Mike: What is your worst memory from school? Was it cross country running in the wet winter?

Jim: Yes, you guessed! Hahaha.

Mike: What is your biggest regret about your school life?

Jim: Not taking enough days off.

Mike: Hahaha. If you could to change one thing, what would you change? More days off?

Jim: I'd changed a lot of the teaching staff.

Mike: Why?

Jim: Old fashioned teaching methods, like "It's your fault if you don't understand that" kind of stuff.

Mike: Oh, times have changed now I think.

Jim: I certainly hope so!

Mike: Thank you.

Jim: No worries.

Exercise

Circle the answer you hear.

Mike: Hi, which high school did you go to?

Folkstone grammar school　　Folkstone high school

Mike: I see. Was it a single sex school or coeducational?

a single sex school　　a coeducational school

Mike: Oh really? How many students were there?

400　　700

Mike: What is your best memory from school?

Being with friends at lunch time

A school trip with friends

Mike: How did you get there?

By train　　By bus

Mike: What sort of sports activities did you do at school?

Basketball　　Hockey

Mike: What is your worst memory from school?

Cross country running　　Math class

Mike: What is your biggest regret about your school life?

Not making many friends　　Not taking more days off

Mike: If you could change one thing, what would you change?

Change a lot of the teachers　　Take more day off

4 Pair work

Interview 2 classmates and write their answer.

Q1. Was your school a single sex or coeducational?

Partner 1 ______________________________

Partner 2 ______________________________

Q2. How many students in that school?

Partner 1 ______________________________

Partner 2 ______________________________

Q3. What is your best memory from high school?

Partner 1 ______________________________

Partner 2 ______________________________

Q4. What is your worst memory from high school?

Partner 1 ____

Partner 2 ____

Q5. What is your biggest regret in life?

Partner 1 ____

Partner 2 ____

Q6. If you could change one thing, what would you change?

Partner 1 ____

Partner 2 ____

Q7. Why?

Partner 1 ____

Partner 2 ____

Q8. ____________________________________? (Make your own question)

Partner 1 ____

Partner 2 ____

5 Dialogue

Read the Dialogue with your partners and answer the questions. (Past tense dialogue and showing one's regret and conditional of wishes or likings (would like to).

Ann: Are you ok, Mr. Kajimoto? You look a bit sad?

Mr. Kajimoto: Oh, Ann! My favorite student nurse! I had the same dream again!

A: You mean the classmate in Santa Monica?

K: Yes, I was trying to smile and talk to her, but my voice had gone and only tears came out, I couldn't stop feeling sad.

A: Oh, that must be terrible...

K: Well, I wish I'd said good-bye to Mary properly. I couldn't face it, so I didn't go and see her. I heard that she had been waiting for me under the clock tower for hours. I stood her up. Then I came to Japan with my family and we lost touch. I wish I could say sorry to her, ask her forgiveness...

A: Do you have her family name and previous address? Would you like me to find her? I can do that with social media!

K: Oh, would you? But I don't have much time left...

Questions

1. Why is Mr. Kajimoto sad?
2. What is his recurrent dream about?
3. What did he do to his friend before he came to Japan?
4. What is his friend's name?
5. What does he want to do?
6. What did Ann offer to Mr. Kajimoto?

6 Short writing exercise

Ann sent an email to her grand-parents in US.

> Hi Grandma & Grandpa!
> How're you doing? It's cold in Japan, not like in Hawaii!
> I'm good! Working at the hospital is fun! But sometimes, kind of sad.
> I miss you both! Love, Ann

Write a short message to your relatives you haven't seen lately. (Grandparents, cousins, aunts and uncles or even old friends like elementary school friends).

7 Quiz

After reading the dialogue, please continue the story using the past tense!
In the story, what did Ann do? What did Mr. Kajimoto do? Did he contact the girl he left when he was in California?
Draw a cartoon!

①	②	③

8 Extra Reading

Well, you don't expect to get much amusement from a visit to A&E, especially after your foot's been run over, but although I was in considerable pain. I did have to laugh at one point.

Of course everybody waiting to be seen is in the same boat, and naturally there is some chat about why you're there. One of the guys I talked to was a builder, he'd stepped on a piece of wood with a nail sticking up and it had gone through his shoe, into his foot, which had swollen right up. That wasn't at all amusing, but we over-head a woman relating the tale of her injury to her neighbor.

Apparently she had been doing some spring-cleaning in her bathroom and unable to reach a spiders web, had stood on the loo seat to try to reach it. Not a good idea as it turned out; the loo seat broke, one leg went down into the pan, her foot stuck in bend as she toppled over backwards......

It feels like it's broken she said, adding that she felt a bit stupid, but that maybe she would be able to laugh about it one day.

Exercise

Answer the following questions.

1. Where is this person?
2. Why he had to laugh?
3. What happened to the woman?

Chapter 13

Tom's friend, Patrick

Tom's friend Patrick came to Japan.

1 Useful Vocabulary

- in hospital
- hundred
- million
- bored
- crazy
- cold
- scary
- out of hospital
- thousand
- billion
- fun
- exciting
- tired
- painful

- more/most
- not as ~ as
- good
- less/least
- expensive
- difficult

2 Grammar

Comparatives

- adjectives with syllable : add ‘er’, ‘r’, + than

short	shorter than	In Canada, summer is shorter than winter.
old	older than	My dad is older than my mom.

- adjectives with 2 or more syllables : add more + than

interesting	more interesting than	I think doing experiments is more interesting than reading about it.
delicious	more delicious than	The pumpkin soup here is more delicious than the asparagus soup.

- adjectives with 2 syllables that end in ‘y’ : change ‘y’ to ‘i’ add ‘er’ + than

easy	easier than	Printing is easier than writing.
happy	happier than	Paul is happier than he was 2 years ago.

- adjectives than end with a single vowel and consonant : double the final letter + er + than (not ‘y’ -grey or ‘w’ slow)

hot	hotter than	It is much hotter in Nagoya than Nagano.
thin	thinner than	She is thinner than she was before the operation.

Superlatives

When using the superlative we use the word ‘the’.
For example-“38.4 is the highest temperature I’ve ever had.”

3 Listening

Dialogue between Tom and Patrick.

Patrick: So how was the hospital, Tom? What was it like compared to your hometown in the UK?

Tom: Well, I had to stay in hospital longer than in the UK. You don't stay in hospital as long as in Japan.

Patrick: So, I guess that was hard.

Tom: Yeah, it was the most difficult part.

Patrick: Worse than the operation?

Tom: Maybe... pain killers are weaker here than in the UK so, it was quite painful.

Patrick: Is your leg still sore now?

Tom: Only a little. It's not as sore as it was a week ago.

Patrick: Great! So, why don't we catch up with friends this evening for dinner?

Tom: Excellent idea. It'll be the most exciting thing I've done in weeks.

Patrick: And, maybe the best food you've had in weeks too.

Read the dialogue in pairs. Discuss the meaning of any words you don't know. What are three differences they talk about in the dialogue.

1. ____________________

2. ____________________

3. ____________________

4 Pair work

Grammar Comparative and superlative

Work with a partner. Choose five words from the list at the back of the book and make your own comparative sentences.

Comparative sentences

1. ____________________

2. ____________________

3. ____________________

4. ____________________

5. ____________________

Superlative sentences

1. ____________________

2. ____________________

3. ____
4. ____
5. ____

Now try flipping the sentences around. Read your sentences out loud in your groups.
Example: I am taller than Lesley.
Flipped : Lesley is shorter than me.
Try making your own "not as ~ as ~" sentences.

5 Blog

Tom's Blog about future trip to South East Asia.

Finally! I have been out of hospital for 7 days now. It seems so long ago that I broke my leg. It is so much better now. It's not as sore as it was two weeks ago. Yes!

The days are getting shorter and soon Christmas will be here. I can't believe that I've been in Japan for a month now. Time flies when you're in hospital…NOT!

My days are more exciting now that I am out of hospital. I'm having more fun with the new friends I made. It's colder than it was when I went into hospital, but the seasons are changing.

It's great to be eating more delicious food too. I think Japanese food is the most delicious I've eaten. Except Natto. I'm not a fan of natto.

I'm feeling much stronger and happier too. I guess I will soon be ready to move on. Time to start planning my next adventure. Going somewhere new…somewhere I've never been…I'll boldly go where no man has ever been… South East Asia, here I come!
Ok.
I know.
I'm not Captain Kirk.

6 Game

Cut the cards. Make two teams. Have two teams come to the board to play Pictionary with the two words. When guessed correctly have the team write a correct sentence on the board using the comparative, superlative or not as ~ as ~ . Some of the words the students can guess easily in Pictionary since they all know the words, but the ones they write will be unknown. Mix them up before the teacher gives them to the students.

Students think of other things to compare and write in the empty boxes.
Look at the back of the book. Page 99.

7 Extra Reading

Now our Tom is well enough to travel again! But has he paid his hospital bill? Let's hope he is covered by his travel insurance!

Cashier: The amount you need to pay for the hospital stay and operation is 25 thousand yen. You pay 30 per cent of the actual cost.
Tom: Wow, that's much cheaper than I thought it would be.
Cashier: Oh, wait. I'm sorry. My mistake. How do you say this number in English - 250 000?
Tom: Actually, it's 250 thousand yen. I like the first number better.
Cashier: I'm sorry, but thank-you for teaching me.

Let's learn numbers

Look at the chart below. Always read the 3 digits first, then read the word at the top of the box.

100 / 10 / 1	100 / 10 / 1	100 / 10 / 1	100 / 10 / 1
billion	million	thousand	(hundred)
0	0	0	0
543	123	789	456

456 = four hundred fifty-six
6,123 = six thousand, one hundred twenty-three.
50,431 = fifty thousand, four hundred thirty-one
980,613,545 = nine hundred eighty million, six hundred thirteen thousand, five hundred forty-five.

Now try to read the number in the third column above.

543,123,789,456
Five hundred forty-three billion, one hundred twenty-three million, seven hundred eighty-nine thousand, four hundred fifty-six.

Pair work

Try writing big numbers. Pass them to a partner and practice saying them.

Chapter 14

Making Suggestions and Experiences

1 Useful Vocabulary

Adverse reactions - (Local, systemic, allergic)

Local reaction: least severe - pain, redness, swelling

Systemic reaction: most frequent - similar to a mild form of the natural disease. (They occur near the middle to the end of the natural diseases usual incubation period. 7-21 days after vaccination)

Allergic reaction - most severe and least common. Difficulty breathing, wheezing, facial swelling

- Hepatitis A
- Thailand
- Last(s) ed
- Let's…

- Tetanus
- Typhoid
- Malaria

- Laos
- Cambodia
- Vietnam

- Go(es) away
- went

- Why don't we…?
- How about…?

② Grammar Focus -Making suggestions

Work with a partner and name as many other countries as you can in 2 minutes. Compare with another pair of students.

③ Dialogue

Listen to the dialogue between Tom and Patrick.
Answer the questions below. Then compare your answer to your partner's.

Tom: Hey, Patrick. Did you check out some of the countries we talked about last week?

Patrick: Yeah, I looked up about Vietnam and Cambodia. I really want to go to Angkor Wat.

Tom: Me too! That sounds great. Can you ride a motorbike?

Patrick: Yeah, I can. I've ridden many bikes. From a 125cc to a 1200cc.

Tom: Then how about renting some motorbikes and riding the Quan Ba Pass or the Ma Pi Leng Pass in Vietnam?

Patrick: Okay! Why don't we go to some beaches as well.

Tom: For sure. Sunshine, beaches, swimming and vitamin D!

Patrick: That would cool, too! Will your leg be okay by then?

Tom: I probably can't do all day hiking but riding is no problem.

Patrick: Awesome.

Questions

What countries did Patrick check out? ______________________________

Can Tom ride a motorbike? ______________________________

What else will they do on their trip? ______________________________

4 Pair work

Make suggestions for a place you and your partner could go to on a trip. Think of some activities you could do there. Use the phrases below. Do a bit of research on the country to help you.

Let's + verb.　　Why don't we + verb?　　How about + verb + ing?

1. ____________________
2. ____________________
3. ____________________
4. ____________________
5. ____________________
6. ____________________

Have you ever + past participle Asking about experiences.

A: Have you ever been to Singapore?

B: Yes, I have lived in Singapore. I lived there for 1 year. I stayed with my friend's family. Have you?

Notice the above sentences. Use the present perfect when talking about experiences. When giving more information use the simple past.

(Note* "ever" is used only in the question. It isn't used in the affirmative answer.)

"Yes, I have ever been to Singapore" **X**

"Yes, I have been to Singapore." **O**

Negative sentences

"No, I've never been to Singapore" OR "No, never."

"No, not yet." Implies you want to or are planning to do something

Work with a partner and ask each other the following. Ask two follow up sentences for each yes answer. Try speaking about each topic for a minute. In the third column, make up your own examples.

Have you ever	… (use the past participle)	Write 5 of your own examples
(Go) abroad	(See) a car accident	
(Get) a vaccination	(Break) a bone	
(Have) a reaction to a vaccination	(Sell) something online	
(Ride) in an ambulance	(Meet) your best friends parents	
(Go) on a cruise	(See) a dolphin in the wild	

5 Blog

Just waiting to finish all my vaccinations before I head off on my next adventure! Whoo hoo! Luckily, I didn't have any adverse reactions to the Typhoid vaccination. Just a localized reaction. I had a bit of redness and swelling at the injection spot. I need to get the rest done soon because it takes about 8 weeks to get them all.

You all know my friend Patrick? He had a rare systemic reaction to the typhoid vaccination. He had stomach cramps and diarrhea so he went to the hospital. It lasted for two days. I hope I don't have any reactions like that and If I do, I hope they go away quickly.

He also has to be careful on our trip to Southeast Asia because he's allergic to bees. He has to carry his epipen with him at all times. Even here in Japan! If he gets stung, he'll go into anaphylactic shock!

Well, I hope I don't need to visit any more hospitals anytime soon. Going 'under the knife' on an operating table was easy but, I don't like these needles. I hate them, in fact. I think I told you before.

Try writing your own blog about a sickness that lasted a long time or any adverse reactions you have had with from a vaccination or a food allergy. If you don't have any experience with the above try writing a blog about any another experience you have had. Give details!

6 Game

Five in a Row

Choose any simple present verbs you have studied so far in this book. Write them in the squares above. Using a coin to flip onto the page. Use the past participle of the verb in a sentence to win the square. The first person with five in a row, horizontally, vertically or diagonally is the winner!

Have the other students decide if the sentence is correct or not.

If you have finished your work, try reading the following. Discuss in small groups.

7 Extra Reading

Travelling can be so much fun! You can have new experiences, meet interesting people and visit amazing new places. Those places might be in your own country or abroad. After I graduated university, I went on a one month trip to four cities in Canada. Quebec City, Montreal, Ottawa and Toronto. In Quebec I met some other Canadians who had never met an English speaking person before. I met them in a local coffee shop. Have you ever tried coffee in a bowl? It’s the usual way to drink coffee there.

After Canada, I went on to travel around South East Asia. I lived in Singapore for a year and made some really great friends. I was still a bit naive and I didn’t think much about vaccinations. I thought I was invincible! I was lucky I didn’t catch anything because I travelled up through Malaysia and Thailand as well. I never got sick, not even once!

But it’s important now to really check out the diseases in a country before you travel. Find the latest data.

In 2017, there was an article published in The Straits Times about ‘A “super malaria” parasite that is spreading through South-east Asia at an alarming rate.’

‘The strain was originally detected in Cambodia in 2007, and experts are calling for action before it reaches other areas such as India or Africa, reported AFP.’

‘“It spread like a wildfire to Vietnam,” said Professor Arjen Dondorp, head of the Oxford Tropical Medicine Research Unit at Mahidol University in Bangkok.’

‘The Lancet Infectious Diseases added: “It started 10 years ago in western Cambodia. It is very fit and spreads very easily. This resistance is taking over. Cambodia already changed to a new drug, likely to last one or two years. Vietnam has to change now.”’

I wonder how far it has spread now? About 10 years ago I heard from my friend in Singapore that his mom had passed away from Malaria. I was in shock. It made me realize how important it is to take precautions against diseases that you may not have in your own country.

But, don’t let the stories stop you from experiencing wonderful adventures of your own! Be safe and be informed.

Chapter 15

Future Plans

1 Useful Vocabulary

- lyrics
- chorus
- graduate
- spring
- days of the week
- holiday
- sleigh bells
- pretend
- poem
- verse
- months of the year
- winter
- weekend
- New year's resolution
- meadow
- lane

2 Grammar Focus

Future 'going to' and 'doing'

We can also use the present continuous for the future when plans are 100% decided.

100%	Be + verb +ing	I am seeing a movie tonight with a friend.
100%	Be going to + verb	I am going to see a movie tonight with a friend.
50~70%	Be thinking of + verb + ing	I am thinking of seeing a movie tonight with a friend.
20~40%	Might + verb	I might see a movie tonight with a friend.
20~40%	Might + be + going + verb	I might be going to see a movie tonight with a friend.

Tone of voice is very important in setting %. A higher, light voice in the "might" will give it a higher percentage. A lower voice with slower, hesitant speech would lower the possibility of "might" .

3 Listening

Listen to the song "Winter Wonderland".

A. Listen and fill in the blanks.

Sleigh bells ________, are you listenin'?
In the _________ snow is glistenin'
A beautiful __________, we're happy tonight
____________ in a winter wonderland.

B. Write the number below beside the words in the boxes.

Gone away is the 1. ______________
Here to stay is the 2. ______________
He sings a love song as we 3. _______________
Walkin' in a winter 4. _______________
In the meadow we can build 5. _______________
Then pretend that he is 6. _______________
He'll say, "Are you married?" We'll say, " 7. _______________

But you can do the job when you're 8. ____________________

• Parson brown	• blue bird
• new bird	• walk along
• in town	• No, man
• wonderland	• a snowman

C. Choose the correct word

Later on we'll *conspire / come fire / aspire* .

As we *team / dream / dreamed* by the fire.

To face unafraid, the *plants / plane / plans* that we've made.

Walking in a *winter's / winner / winter* wonderland.

Practice the pronunciation of the "ing" words in the song above. It's very common to drop the last 'g'.

What are some other Christmas songs that you know? Do you like singing? Did you get a present from Santa when you were a child? Until what age did you believe in Santa? Discuss freely in groups of 3 or 4 people.

4 Pair work

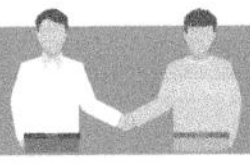

Read the questions below. Make up three future questions of your own.

Interview 2 classmates. 'Answer more' for each question. Write your partners answers.

Q1. What are you doing this weekend?

Partner 1 ______________________________

Partner 2 ______________________________

Q2. What are you going to do for Christmas?

Partner 1 ______________________________

Partner 2 ______________________________

Q3. What are you going to do December 31st?

Partner 1 ______________________________

Partner 2 ______________________________

Q4. Do you have any plans for winter holiday?

Partner 1 ______________________________

Partner 2 ______________________________

Q5. Are you giving anyone a Christmas present?

Partner 1 ______________________________

Partner 2 ______________________________

Q6. How much are going to get for New Year's money?

Partner 1 ______________________________

Partner 2 ______________________________

Q7. What are you planning to do after you graduate?

Partner 1 ______________________________

Partner 2 ______________________________

Write your own Questions for 8-10

Q8. ______________________________?

Partner 1 ______________________________

Partner 2 ______________________________

Q9. ______________________________?

Partner 1 ______________________________

Partner 2 ______________________________

Q10. ______________________________?

Partner 1 ______________________________

Partner 2 ______________________________

5 Blog

Soon to be HAPPY NEW YEAR. I'm thinking of what my new year's resolution is going to be... I still have time to decide.

But now - Christmas in Japan! I'm missing my family a bit. Hey mom! Hey, dad! And a "hey" to my little sister. I love you guys. I'm going to hang out with my friends on the 25th. We're exchanging presents at a restaurant. It's going to be a lot of fun. BUT - Christmas Eve is a couple's night. It's a romantic evening with your 'special someone.' I don't have a special someone... hmm. I might head out to a bar for a few drinks with friends.
No! I know. I'm going to have a get together at my place with some of the people I met at the hospital. Good plan! It's decided then. If anyone reading this wants to come, leave a comment.
I'm giving a present to the nurse, Ann, to say thank you. She helped me so much during my hospital stay. Let me know if you have any ideas of what to get for her. I have no idea.

6 Games

CHARADES OR PICTIONARY
Make two teams and think of some short phrases or words to describe the winter and the New Year's season.
Eg. Snowman, winter wonderland, Christmas Eve, New Year's money etc.
Pass the words and phrases that you wrote to the other team. Use the words to play a game of Charades or Pictionary. Don't make the phrases too difficult!

Play regular charades or have a relay with the Charades game. The team that guesses all their hints and finishes first is the winner. The teacher needs to monitor the two teams to make sure the person doing the acting isn't speaking. Alternatively, have the teams take turns to do the acting and time it.

HOLIDAY TALENT SHOW

Each student must prepare a small reading, a song, a joke, a poem, etc. to give to the entire class. It should have a 'wintery' theme. Have fun and enjoy the show! Don't panic.

WRITE YOUR OWN HAIKU

Describe holidays, playing outside, a favorite cozy activity, getting dressed in layers—whatever you feel comfortable with. The 5-7-5 line poem may be a challenge but let's see what you can come up with. Again, have fun with it!

7 Reading comprehension

The song may sound happy and joyful but, the story behind this popular song isn't as happy as you might think.

A man named Richard Smith who lived in Honesdale, Pennsylvania, wrote a poem about a carefree, fun day in the snow. Looking out his window, he saw children playing in the park. He wished he could play outside as the children were doing but, he couldn't. He was suffering from tuberculosis. Tuberculosis was also called 'consumption'. It was a highly contagious disease that primarily affected the lungs. It also caused other body tissue to waste away. It was the most common cause of death in the 19th century.

Richard Smith showed his poem, "Winter Wonderland", to his friend Felix Bernard. Felix was a Jewish musician. He composed a melody to go along with the poem. Many Christmas songs were written and/or composed by Jewish musicians.

Sadly, Richard Smith died in 1935, at the age of 34. He died the day before his 34th birthday. Some reports say he died before he could hear the music Felix Bernard made for "Winter Wonderland". Other reports say Richard Smith lived long enough to hear Guy Lombard and his orchestra, the Royal Canadians, perform his song the Christmas before he died.

The classic recording of the song "Winter Wonderland" by Guy Lombardo and the Royal Canadians, made in New York City on October 29, 1934,

To this day the song been covered by over 200 artists, including Bing Crosby, Andrea Bocelli, Dolly Parton, Dean Martin, Elvis, Aretha Franklin and Bob Dylan. Have you ever heard this song?

Exercise

Read the above and check anything you don't understand with a partner. Answer the questions below. Check your answers with your partner.

1. Who wrote the poem, "Winter Wonderland" and where did he live ?

____

2. Who composed the melody?

____

3. When did Richard Smith die?

____

4. What did he die from?

____

In UK —Epilogue

Dialogue

Tom wants to tell Ann about his big news.

Tom: Ann-over here! Great to see you, really glad you came! How've you been?

Ann: So good to see you, Tom. I've really been looking forward to seeing you. I'm a bit exhausted, but it's been great. My first time in the UK. You said you've got some big news to tell me - you're not getting married are you ?

Tom: Hahaha.... nothing like that.... it's that I've decided that I want to go into nursing. After my time in hospital, on my travels I thought a lot about what I wanted to do with my life.

Ann: Wow, that's fantastic!

Tom: I wanted to save it to tell you in person. Do you think that you could help me with some of the basics? I don't have much of a clue about medical things, but I'd really like to help people.

Ann: Of course, I'd love to help you. I've got a lot of basic information with me as we've exams when I get back. We can start any time, if you're not busy we can go to my hotel and I'll copy anything you think might be helpful for you.

Cats	Lexus	
Dogs	Hyundai	
July	Whales	
December	Dolphins	
Cars	Watermelon	
Bullet trains	Durian	
McDonald’s	Television	
Mos Burger	Youtube	
Chinese	Students	
English	Teachers	

索引

NDC 490　107 p　26 cm

英《えい》語《ご》で学《まな》ぶプライマリーケア

Primary Care — A practical English communication course for Nurses and healthcare workers

2020 年 7 月 22 日　第 1 刷発行

編著者　西牟田《ニシムタ》 祐美子《ユミコ》
発行者　渡瀬昌彦
発行所　株式会社 講談社
〒112-8001　東京都文京区音羽 2-12-21
販　売　(03)5395-4415
業　務　(03)5395-3615
編　集　株式会社　講談社サイエンティフィク
代表　堀越俊一
〒162-0825　東京都新宿区神楽坂 2-14　ノービィビル
編　集　(03)3235-3701

本文データ制作　株式会社 双文社印刷
カバー・表紙印刷　豊国印刷 株式会社
本文印刷・製本　株式会社 講談社

落丁本・乱丁本は，購入書店名を明記のうえ，講談社業務宛にお送りください．送料小社負担にてお取替えします．なお，この本の内容についてのお問い合わせは講談社サイエンティフィク宛にお願いいたします．
定価はカバーに表示してあります．

Printed in Japan

ISBN 978-4-06-520090-2